A HISTORICAL STUDY

OF

THE MIGRANT IN CALIFORNIA

A Thesis

The University of Southern California

by

J. Donald Fisher

1945

Reprinted in 1973 by

R AND E RESEARCH ASSOCIATES

4843 Mission St., San Francisco 94112

18581 McFarland Ave., Saratoga, CA 95070

Publishers and Distributors of Ethnic Studies

Editor: Adam S. Eterovich

Publisher: Robert D. Reed

Library of Congress Card Catalog Number

73-78057

ISBN

0-88247-225-9

PREFACE

The decade of the 1930's was one of great unrest, and especially so in California. Here, in addition to the great economic problems facing the rest of the world, was the added problem brought about by the great number of newcomers to the state.

California had experienced migrations throughout much of her history, but never before under such economic conditions. This new migration, consisting largely of which Americans, created in addition a social problem.

The problem of the migration to California and of the migratory workers in the state drew the attention of the American public. Hundreds of articles appeared in magazines of nation-wide circulation. A special congressional committee was appointed to investigate the problem. One of the "best-selling" novels of the period was concerned with migrants to, and in, California.

This study attempts to make possible a clearer understanding of the migration to California during the 1930's through a presentation of the historical background which made possible the situation which obtained. This includes a short study of the land system, the types of migratory laborers formerly found in California, sources of the recent migration, direct and contributing causes of the migration, and some of the effects of this migration to California.

A careful search was made to find and read all available, pertinent, contemporary writings published in magazine or book form. This material was, in many cases, written with a bias--sometimes slight and sometimes deep. Many published and unpublished reports by government agencies were studied. Personal contact was made with large numbers of migrants, and trips were made through the region from which many of these people came and the regions in which they worked after coming to California.

Much valuable material was secured through the kindness of the Farm Security Administration, Region IX, through the San Francisco office.

Especially appreciated was the guidance and encouragement of Doctor Owen C. Coy, for without his stimulating interest the work would have been abandoned, Doctor Frank H. Garver, and Doctor John E. Nordskog who patiently served as the supervising committee.

TABLE OF CONTENTS

LIST OF TABLES

CHAPTER I

THE DEVELOPMENT OF AGRICULTURE IN CALIFORNIA

California, during its Spanish and Mexican periods, was a vast pastoral land. The only planting which was done was for the purpose of sustenance of the inhabitants.[1] The means and implements used were very crude. The Spanish ranchero could not be bothered with such rude labor and this work was delegated to the Indians, who had been trained in it by the mission fathers. No one thought of raising grain for the horses and cattle--they could secure a hazardous and meagre living from the open range.

THE SPANISH AND MEXICAN LAND GRANTS

Southern California is well known as a region of great Spanish land grants. The policy of making such grants was continued under the Mexican regime, and was extended to other parts of California.

The first white man to make his home in the San Joaquin Valley region was Jose Noriega, who was granted the Los Meganos Rancho in 1836 and sold it to Dr. John Marsh in 1838.[2] This rancho consisted of 17,712 acres between Mount Diablo and Brentwood, and was watered by the San Joaquin River. Twenty-nine other large grants were made by Mexican governors, ranging from more than 8,000 to more than 100,000 acres in a tract, and as much as 500,000 acres to one individual.[3] This was the beginning of the vast empires still owned by individuals or corporations in this part of California.

THE AMERICAN PERIOD

With the coming of the foreigners in increasing numbers in the decade prior to the American occupation of California, we find renewed signs of agricultural development. Sutter was the pioneer in this field, when he opened his great plantations on the Sacramento in 1840, and trained Indians to cultivate them. Sutter's work resulted in an agricultural development of the country from the Stanislaus to the Russian River by foreigners, mostly Americans, within the next few years.[4]

The discovery of gold in 1848 brought a great influx of population in the famous Gold Rush of '49. With an increasing population[5] there was, of course, a greatly increased demand for food-stuffs. This demand brought large profits to the California farmer. As a result, many of those who had come to dig, or wash, gold turned to agriculture after an unsuccessful season or two.[6] Vegetables, potatoes, and grain were raised in large quantities, and by 1854 the state was almost self-supporting again.

Among those who came to San Francisco in the gold era were two butchers who were to figure in the story of California for a century--for their names are still widely known. Miller and Lux, as they were known, started independently, but soon teamed up as two of the great landholders of the country. Both were dissatisfied with the beef they were able to purchase and decided to raise their own cattle.[7] Starting with the purchase of a rancho, they took advantage of the Swamp Land Act of 1850 which provided that anyone who would purchase swamp land at a price of $1.25 per acre and then spent an equal amount in reclaiming the land and making it useful farm land would be refunded the full purchase price. Skillful management enabled them to rapidly build up vast estates.

The great central valley, especially the San Joaquin where rainfall was extremely light, was considered an arid waste in the early period, but as agriculture began to develop it was found that very fine crops of grain could be raised. Due to this development California became one of the great wheat-raising states for a number of years. It was possible to export grain crops profitably, as grain would stand the long sea voyage, and rates were favorable due to the great excess of imports over exports. Improved farm land increased from only 32,454 acres in 1850 to 2,468,034 acres in 1860, and 6,218,133 acres in 1870.[8]

This early demand for wheat, and the great acreages available, resulted in the invention of the Stockton Gang Plow in 1860.[9] In turn, the development of this means of plowing huge tracts brought about a demand for a better means of planting, and the broadcast seeder was invented in 1867.

Improved means of preparation of soil and planting made necessary a better means of harvesting, as it was then possible to plant more than could be harvested, but by 1900 the average horse-drawn combined harvester could harvest from twenty-five to forty-five acres a day.[10]

As early as 1886, wheat fields of 10,000 to 30,000 acres were planted in the Fresno and Tulare regions. Railway stations, which later became sites of the towns of the valley, were established at the chief loading points for wheat.[11]

With the coming of the railroad a great new opportunity was opened for California agriculture, as now crops which were of a perishable nature could be shipped to the eastern markets. The ability to ship these foods was greatly increased in 1888 by the introduction of the refrigerator car. Crops other than grain, however, required water.

Irrigation had been introduced in California in the early years of the missions, but only on a small scale. After the decline of the missions, little further was done to develop irrigation systems until 1870. The first extensive development was made in the San Joaquin Valley between 1871 and 1878 by capitalists who had extensive holdings in the valley.[12] After great difficulty was encountered, the company quit and sold to Miller and Lux[13] for a third of the money already spent.[14] The work was then continued by them until 190,000 acres of the San Joaquin were being irrigated by 1880 at a water cost of about $1.50 per acre. Other developments had to wait for government assistance. The growth of irrigation projects has continued to the present time. The research of C.R. Niklason shows an increase in irrigation enterprises in California from $72,580,000 in 1910, to $450,968,000 in 1930. There was also an increase in average annual cost per acre from $1.54 to $6.10 during that period.[15]

The development of irrigation made possible the extension of vegetable raising and the introduction of fruit raising on a large scale. It also resulted in the introduction of cotton and other crops which require great amounts of labor during a portion of the year. These high labor crops, however, do not require the steady employment of labor, but are seasonal in demand. This factor has been responsible for much of the agricultural labor problem in California.

Footnotes--Chapter I

[1] H. H. Bancroft, *History of California,* VII, 1.

[2] Wallace Smith, *Garden of the Sun,* 76.

[3] Smith, *Garden of the Sun,* 87.

[4] Bancroft, *History,* VII, 2.

[5] The population in January, 1849, was estimated as 26,000. The U.S. Census gave 92,000 in 1850 and 380,000 in 1860.

[6] Bancroft, *History,* VII, 2.

[7] Smith, *Garden,* 193.

[8] United States, Bureau of the Census, *Ninth Census: 1870,* III, iii, 81-91.

[9] Smith, *Garden,* 222.

[10] Ibid., 238.

[11] Ibid., 244.

[12] Bancroft, *History,* VII, 9.

[13] cf. ante, 3.

[14] Smith, op. cit., 195.

[15] C.R. Niklason, *Commercial Survey of the Pacific Southwest.*

CHAPTER II

TYPES OF MIGRANT LABORERS IN CALIFORNIA

It is easy to assume that migrant workers are necessarily agricultural laborers, but that is not always true. Frequently, however, migrants who were formerly engaged in other pursuits do become agricultural workers through availability of that type of work. Such people usually provide the cheapest sort of labor.

THE CHINESE

With the introduction of intensive farming, which required large amounts of hand labor (which must necessarily be cheap labor, to insure a profit), the early farmer naturally turned to the most readily available source--the Chinese.[1]

The first Chinese immigrants to come to California were two men and one woman who came to San Francisco in 1848. The two men immediately went to the mines, but the woman remained as a servant in a family who had recently come to San Francisco from Hong Kong, China. There were soon great additions to this original trio. In February, 1849, there were fifty-four Chinese men in California, and by August, 1852, there were 18,026 men and fourteen women. The rapidity of this immigration can best be seen in Table I.[2]

Table I

Chinese in California

	Men	Women
February 1849	54	0
January 1850	787	2
January 1851	4,018	7
January 1852	7,512	8
May 1852	11,787	7
August 1852	18,026[3]	14

When the labor trouble began in 1876 there were approximately 116,000 Chinese in California, of whom possibly 6,000 were women. It was estimated that there were about 151,000 Chinese in the United States at that time.[4]

The Chinese immigrants were imported by the "Six Companies"--Chinese organizations which contracted to pay the passage for the immigrants in return for not only interest on their money, but a percentage of the earnings of the immigrant for years to come.

Race feeling first became noticeable in 1852. At that time there was an attempt to create a coolie system to take the place of slavery. Under this system the Chinese would be regarded as permanent "apprentices."[5] Organized labor held a racial feeling to the extent that there was no attempt made by the unions to organize the Chinese.[6] In 1852 we also find the first attempt to exclude the Chinese from California. By 1855 exorbitant rates were being charged the Chinese for the privilege of mining. This, together with the extortion of the "Companies," caused many to return to China.[7]

With the beginning of the railroads, several thousands of Chinese were given employment as construction laborers. In this way costs of construction were cut considerably, as lower rates of pay were possible. After the completion of the railroads, many were employed as section hands in the maintenance of the railroads.

As it was found to be impracticable to return the Chinese to China, due to the large numbers,[8] the possibility was seen of utilizing this source of cheap labor to develop the country. They were used, therefore, for digging ditches, building roads, and such public works. With the development of the demand for agricultural produce this was seen as the means of quickly and cheaply developing the agricultural industry, as there was insufficient white help available, and that which was available demanded a much higher wage than it was possible for the infant industry to afford.[9]

The Chinese took up gardening, farming, viticulture, horticulture, laundrying, cooking, and general housework, and monopolized them to some extent. They were employed by the railroads, both in construction and maintenance, in lumbering, and in the great fisheries. They even took up shoemaking and cigar manufacturing.[10] In these ways they played an important part in the industrial and commercial development of California. They were opposed, naturally, as is any source of cheap labor, but much of the early opposition came from those who also were immigrants, and who, now that they were in a new land to which they had come for its freedom, wanted to show their authority.[11]

Finally, the Treaty of 1881 with China resulted in the passing of an act, on

May 6, 1882, which suspended Chinese immigration for ten years. This act, however, had the immediate effect of raising the wage level of the Chinese, as they refused to work at former rates due to limitation of competition.[12]

The number of Chinese laborers in California remained quite constant for many years. The census of 1900 reported 40,262 Chinese in California, but this figure was admittedly too low. As was stated in the United States Immigration Reports for 1907-1910: "it being ... almost impossible to enumerate all ... of the foreign-born males living under such conditions as ... found among the Chinese."[13]

Gradually the Chinese drifted to the cities or became their own bosses. They farmed for themselves, and by their methods raised the productivity of the soil, which in turn raised the price of land.[14] All agricultural labor camps maintained by growers of labor contractors were subject to inspection during occupancy by the State Commission of Immigration and Housing. By 1914 only 2.3 per cent of the population in these camps were Chinese, according to the inspection reports.[15] In 1920 they were "no longer serious competitors," and by 1930 they constituted only 0.5 per cent of the labor camp population. The decline in numbers of Chinese laborers was due to several factors: (1) the drift to the cities; (2) the age of the Chinese, who had not been replenished due to the immigration laws; and, (3) the fact that the second generation Chinese were unsatisfactory workers, due to the rapid rise in living standards of the Chinese in the United States;[16] and, (4) the return of many Chinese to China in the twentieth century.[17]

THE JAPANESE

The Japanese first appeared in California agriculture at Vacaville, where they worked as fruit pickers, in 1890.[18] By 1895 they had spread as far south as Fresno--the point at which the Chinese stopped.

The Japanese did not become a factor of importance in California until the beginning of the present century, when the Chinese began to be a rapidly declining available labor supply for agriculture. In 1900 there were only 24,326 Japanese in the entire United States, 10,151 of whom were in California.[19]

Before 1898 the number of Japanese reaching continental United States never totaled as many as 2,000 in any year, but in 1900 the number of newly-arrived Japanese coming from Canada, Mexico, and Japan was 12,626. In 1905, however, this number dropped to 4,319, about half of whom came to Hawaii rather than the mainland. Between 1902 and 1907, about 37,000 Japanese came from Hawaii to the west coast.[20]

Beginning in 1907, by mutual agreement between the United States and Japan, passports were to be granted by Japan only to laborers who had been residents of the United States and were returning, and to "non-laborers." While the agreement was not strictly observed it did tend to limit immigration of new Japanese, although large numbers of wives and children came after 1907.[21]

After 1908 Japanese immigration became negligible, when compared with the number of emigrants. There was a net decrease in Japanese of 2,440 for the years 1909-1910, but a net surplus of immigrants from Japan each year after 1910, until 1925.[22] Beginning with 1925--the year following the passing of the Exclusion Act-- there has been greater emigration than immigration each year.[23]

The Japanese immigrants did not all come directly to the United States from Japan. Many of them came from Hawaii, Mexico, or British Columbia, where they had lived for some years. These immigrants were mostly of the agricultural class, being small farmers of farm laborers.

The sugar beet industry and vegetable growing had developed on a hugh scale in the Sacramento and San Joaquin valleys by 1909. As yet there was no large stable population in the valleys. This situation led to an extraordinary demand for migratory labor. The Chinese had by this time become less important in the labor situation, and the Japanese filled the cheap labor gap which was left by the Chinese. It was estimated 30,000 Japanese were then engaged as agricultural laborers in California. They performed practically all the hand work in the berry patches, two-thirds of that in the sugar beet fields, one-half of the hand work in the vineyards, and slightly less in vegetables and orchards.[24]

The availability of this cheap labor helped agriculture along its path toward intensified farming which demands great amounts of seasonal labor.

Development of intensified agriculture brought with it the introduction of packing houses, canneries, and wineries, to care for the crops raised. These related industries, like agriculture, also demand huge amounts of labor for a short season of the year.

The Japanese spread rapidly over the entire state, becoming the first Asiatic laborers in the citrus fruit of Southern California.[25] By 1909 they constituted half the orange pickers in this area. They were used to undermine the wage rate, although they were not as satisfactory to the grower in that respect as had been the Chinese in the north and central parts of the state at an earlier period.

As early as 1910 a resentment had developed against the Japanese even stronger than was ever felt toward the Chinese. This resentment had several bases.[26] First, although Japanese were unorganized, they walked off the job if they became dissatisfied. They also banded together and threatened to strike if they decided the wages were too low.

Second, the Japanese tended to establish themselves on an independent basis. They acquired land, and intensified cultivation even further than had the Chinese before them. In this way they, like the Chinese, raised the price of land and stood in the way of the small American farmer.

Third, the growing independence of the Japanese deprived the large landowner of his cheap labor market.

An example of the feeling in the state is shown in the report of the State Labor Commissioner of May 30, 1910.[27] He stated that labor of the Japanese-Chinese type was essential for the development and perpetuation of the fruit and vegetable industries in California. It was his belief that the use of white labor was impracticable due to the economic conditions necessary for this class of labor. He further stated that the transition from cereal growing to specialized agriculture increased the demand for temporary help beyond the normal available supply within the state, even during the periods of largely increasing population. He rated the Chinese as the best laborer of the type needed, with the Japanese in second place.

A reply to the above report was published by Chester H. Rowell in the editorial columns of the Fresno Republican under the title, "A Calamity." Mr. Rowell attacked the report as giving official recognition to the doctrine of servile labor. He said that according to the report, California cannot raise both fruit and American civilization, and as fruit is more important, civilization must be sacrificed. Mr.

Rowell declared that the California farmer preferred his laborers to be slaves, or worse. He pleaded for raising the economic condition of the agricultural laborer, and for the use of Mexicans,[28] in the period of adjustment to a higher economic status for the laborer which would allow the use of white American labor.[29]

The anti-alien land laws which were passed in 1913 in an attempt to protect the small American farmer from the Japanese were circumvented by the large land-holders by leasing, or selling, to the Japanese through his American-born child.[30]

Reports of the State Board of Control show that in 1915 the Japanese controlled agricultural products to a great extent. This is shown in Table II.[31]

Table II

Japanese Control in Agriculture
1915

Product	Per Cent
Berries	88
Sugar Beets	67
Nursery Products	58
Grapes	52
Vegetables	46
Citrus Fruits	39
Deciduous Fruits	36

As the Alien Land Laws were enforced more closely, many Japanese moved into the cities, and those who remained in agriculture tended to be employed by their fellow countrymen. The Mexican and Filipino were also being introduced in an effort to again lower the wage scale, as the Japanese were rapidly improving their standard of living and did not hesitate to demand higher wages.[32] Finally, the Immigration Act of 1924, which definitely excludes Japanese as well as Chinese because of their ineligibility to citizenship, put an end to further immigration of Japanese laborers.

The rapid decline in the importance of the Japanese as a source of migratory labor can be most easily seen in the table below (page 11).[33]

THE SOUTHERN EUROPEANS

Southern Europeans began to be a factor in the agricultural labor market in California at the beginning of this century, about the time the Japanese influx was

Table III

Percentage of Japanese in the California Labor Camp Population

Year	Per Cent
1914	7.4
1920	5.6
1924	4.5
1928	3.4
1930	1.9

beginning to be noticed.

Most of the Europeans were absorbed in the East in industry, at least temporarily, and in this way had assimilated enough to raise their standards of living to a station much higher than that of the Oriental before reaching the west coast. This higher standard of living made the European immigrant unavailable as a source of "cheap" labor.

The southern European did, however, become a big factor in migratory agricultural labor. The Italians, especially, became one of the largest single sources of this type of labor, as is shown in Table IV.[34]

Table IV

Percentage of Italians, Spanish, and Portuguese in
the California Labor Camp Population

Year	Total	Italian	Portuguese	Spanish
1914	15.9%	12.8%	1.6%	1.5%
1915	16.3	10.4	2.7	3.2
1920	8.4	4.4	1.7	2.3
1922	8.7	4.8	1.9	2.0
1924	7.3	3.2	2.0	2.1
1926	7.1	2.5	2.0	2.6
1927	6.0	2.3	1.6	2.1
1928	4.7	2.0	1.1	1.6
1929	3.8	1.4	1.2	1.2
1930-31	3.0	1.5	.6	.9
1931-32	2.8	.7	1.0	1.1
1932-33	2.5	.5	.7	1.3
1933-34	3.2	.5	.7	2.0

The Europeans, even more than the Japanese, became land owners. This is indicated by the rapidly declining percentage of this group in the labor camps, as shown above, and is borne out by the 1920 census which showed 4,453 Italian-born farm operators in California. The same census showed 3,400 Portuguese-born farm operators in California. Those who did not become farm operators tended to work as regular hands for their countrymen, rather than as migratory laborers.[35]

THE MEXICAN

The Mexican population is one of different races. According to the Mexican census of 1928 only 9.8 per cent of the population is white; 59.3 per cent is mestizo; 29.2 per cent is Indian; 1.0 per cent is of other races, unclassified; and 0.7 per cent is foreign born.[36] Dr. George P. Clements of the Los Angeles Chamber of Commerce stated that the Mexicans who come to the United States are peons, or Indians, as primitive as those in America at the time the first colonists arrived.[37]

Shortly after the beginning of the present century the Mexican began to be a source of labor available to the California farmer. These Mexicans, originally from the interior of Mexico, were brought into the northern part of that country to work on the railways, in mines, and in smelters. When these Mexicans learned that wages were much higher in the United States, large numbers of them came into this country through El Paso, Texas, where they were hired to the railroads. The railroads were greatly pleased with this new source of labor, as they were able to lower the prevailing wages. The Mexicans were transported to their new places of residence without charge by those railroads whose lines entered El Paso, and at party rates by the others. By 1909 the Santa Fe and Southern Pacific lines employed Mexicans, exclusively, as section hands on their southern lines.[38]

By that time the Mexicans made up one-sixth of the sugar beet workers in California, but had not become of any importance in any other branch of agriculture. There were a few hundred employed in grape picking around Fresno, Tulare, and Visalia, but the rest were in Southern California.

In 1908, approximately one-third of the persons given assistance in the county of Los Angeles were Mexicans, although they constituted only about one-twentieth of the population of that county.

While Southern California by 1908 was already feeling the effects of the Mexican immigration, as noted, it was not until during World War I that the immigration

12

became so heavy as to cause concern to the state as a whole. The heavy influx, beginning in 1918, was apparently due to the prevailing shortage of labor due to the war.[39]

As the Mexicans would work for the lowest wage of any laborers, and their migratory nature made them easily available, they were eagerly sought by the farmers. While the Mexicans were employed as agricultural laborers, the majority of the Mexican immigrants were unskilled but not agricultural laborers.[40]

Table V shows the number of Mexicans legally admitted into the United States between 1909 and 1929, who declared California to be their intended residence. This clearly pictures the sudden increase in Mexican immigration beginning in 1918.[41]

Table V

Mexicans Legally Entering the United States to
Reside in California

1909-11	1,973
1912-14	2,579
1915-17	3,217
1918-20	10,100
1921-23	15,210
1924-26	27,722
1927-29	30,998
Total	91,799

By 1928 the Mexican problem was causing some concern in California. In an attempt to secure the facts relating to the industrial, social and agricultural aspects of this problem, a committee was appointed by Governor C. C. Young on March 28, 1928. They made a thorough study, and completed their report in September, 1930.

The United States Census had not as yet made any count of the Mexican-born residents of this country, but the committee appointed by Governor Young estimated the number in California for the ten-year periods, beginning 1890, as follows:[42]

Table VI

Mexicans in California

1890	7,164
1900	8,086
1910	33,694
1920	88,771
1930	234,000

13

That these estimates must be fairly conservative is witnessed by the estimate of 82,119 for 1920, made by the United States Census Bureau in 1930,[43] and by the actual count of Mexican-born residents of California in 1930 of 368,013.[44]

It should be understood that the number of Mexicans as shown in Table V are by no means all of the Mexicans who entered California during the period. Many came from Arizona and Texas--particularly from Texas--and many more "just crossed the border" in order to escape payment of the eight dollars per head tax.[45]

No figures are available to show the number of Mexicans employed as agricultural laborers, or migratory workers, but a census of the labor camp population as taken by the Department of Immigration and Housing shows the percentage of Mexicans in the labor camps for the various years:[46]

Table VII

Percentage of Mexicans in the California
Labor Camp Population

Year	Per Cent
1915	7.1
1920	14.0
1924	13.6
1928	28.9
1931-32	28.2
1933-34	32.5

By 1930 the Mexicans were the largest group of non-European immigrants in California.

The following table of racial data for California, taken from the 1930 Census, shows the significance of the groups of laborers in this study in relation to the total population of the state.[47] (See Table VIII, page 15)

THE HINDU

While the Hindu has been mentioned frequently as a factor in the agricultural labor field in California, there has always been a negligible supply of this group. The years 1907, 1908, and 1910 were the only ones in which Hindu immigration exceeded 1,000.[48]

The net excess of Hindu immigrants to the United States (over Hindus

Table VIII

Population in California by Race, 1930

Total Population	Number	Per Cent
Total	5,677,251	100.0
White	5,040,247	88.8
Mexican	368,013	6.5
Japanese	97,456	1.7
Negro	81,048	1.4
Chinese	37,361	.7
Filipino	30,470	.5
Indian	19,212	.3
Hindu	1,873	*
Korean	1,097	*
Other	474	*

*less than 0.1 per cent not indicated

departed) from 1900 to 1920 was only 3,733. The Immigration Act of 1917 stopped further immigration of Hindu laborers.

There were probably never more than 3,000 Hindus in the state of California. The 1930 Census showed 1,873.[49] These laborers worked in agriculture and in the lumber industry, but prejudice was always great against them. They are mentioned here only because of the popular belief that they have been a factor in the agricultural labor supply in California.

THE FILIPINO

The last important source of foreign labor for California agriculture was the Filipino. This new source of labor did not appear until after 1920, and was not important until 1923 when 2,426 Filipinos were admitted into California. From that year on, there were large numbers of new immigrants each year.

The increase in Filipino residents in California is shown when it is noted that in 1910 there were only five Filipinos in the state; in 1920 there were 2,674; and in 1930 the number had increased to 30,470. The growth in percentage of Filipino laborers in the labor camps is also presented, as it showed the rapid increase in Filipino agricultural labor of the migratory type:[50] (Table IX - page 16)

Table IX

Percentage of Filipinos in the California Labor Camp Population

Year	Per Cent
1920	less than 0.5
1922	0.5
1924	2.9
1926	5.3
1928	6.3
1930-31	9.8
1931-32	13.6
1932-33	11.1
1933-34	11.3

The Filipino laborer was used principally on large farms. In the period 1930 - 1940 almost all of the asparagus work was done by Filipinos (about 6,000 workers), while they were also employed in fruit picking, rice harvesting, hoeing and topping sugar beets, lettuce harvesting, grape picking, celery planting, hop picking, and for general ranch labor.[51] The wages paid to the Filipinos were the lowest paid to any migratory workers in that period. This was possible, as they were almost entirely a group of single males who lived together in groups.

That the Filipino was one of the important groups of migratory workers is shown by the figures of the California Division of Immigration and Housing in the 1938 report which showed that Filipinos (in the northern section of California) did 90 per cent of the work in asparagus. Combined with the Japanese, as Orientals, they did 20 per cent of the work in peaches, 50 per cent of the work in pears, 90 per cent of the work in grapes, and all of the work in celery and miscellaneous vegetables.[52]

THE NATIVE WHITE--"DUST-BOWLERS," OR "OKIES"

Beginning about 1930 a new and rapidly increasing source of migratory workers appeared in California. These were the white Americans. For a few years these migrants were largely single men, but beginning in 1935 there was a tremendous influx of families. At last California had a source of white agricultural labor supply.

This situation was not brought about by a sudden decision on the part of California farmers that it would be nobler to promote American civilization than to make a profit at the expense of laborers of lower standards of living.[53]

It was the result of several factors which brought about a great migration of Americans from their former homes in the central and other regions.

Due to the fact that a greater number of these migrants originated in Oklahoma than elsewhere, and to the popular belief that the drought of 1934 was the reason for migration, the names "Okies," and "Dust-bowlers," were commonly used in speaking of these refugees.

Footnotes--Chapter II

[1] Bancroft, History of California, VII, 336.

[2] Ibid.

[3] Note the sudden rapid increase during the year 1852. 476 had died or returned to China.

[4] Bancroft, loc. cit.

[5] Ibid.

[6] California, State Relief Administration, Migratory Labor in California, 17.

[7] Bancroft, op. cit., 338.

[8] Ibid., 339. It would have taken five vessels per month for four years to return the Chinese to China.

[9] Bancroft, op. cit., 339.

[10] Ibid., 342.

[11] Ibid., 340.

[12] Ibid., 348.

[13] U.S., 61st Congress, 3d Session, Senate, Report of the Immigration Commission, I, 654.

[14] California, SRA, Migratory Labor, 17.

[15] Ibid., 18. From the records of the State Commission of Immigration and Housing. These records were not available.

[16] Calif., SRA, op. cit., 18.

[17] E. G. Mears, Resident Orientals on the American Pacific Coast, 408. Shows a net loss of 9,251 Chinese in the U.S., 1900-1926, due to excess of emigration over immigration. Deaths were not included in net loss shown.

[18] Calif., SRA, op. cit., 21.

[19] U.S., Bureau of the Census, Twelfth Census: 1900, I, i.

[20] U.S., 61st Congress, 3d Session, Senate, Report of the Immigration Commission, I, 660.

[21] Ibid.

[22] Mears, Resident Orientals, 409.

[23] U.S., Department of Labor, Bureau of Immigration, Annual report of Commissioner-General of Immigration, fiscal years 1924-25 to 1930-31.

[24] Calif., SRA, Migratory Labor in California, 20.

[25] The Chinese had not penetrated further south than Fresno as agricultural laborers.

[26] Calif., SRA, op. cit., 21-22.

[27] Mears, Resident Orientals, 444-445. Select Documents. Reprint of news item from the Fresno Republican, May 30, 1910.

[28] This was at the beginning of the period in which the Mexican was the important source of agricultural labor.

[29] Mears, Resident Orientals, 446-448. Select Documents. Editorial, Fresno Republican, May 30, 1910.

[30] Calif., SRA, Migratory, op. cit., 23.

[31] Calif., Board of Control, California and the Oriental. Report to Governor Stephens, June 19, 1920.

[32] This was one of the earliest complaints against the Japanese by their employers. Cf. ante, 16.

[33] Calif., SRA, Migratory Labor in California, 24. Compiled from the camp inspection records of the State Commission of Immigration and Housing. Practically all labor camps in use at that time were included, as all grower and labor contractor camps for migratory workers were subject to inspection during occupancy.

[34] Calif., SRA, Migratory, op. cit., 25.

[35] U.S., Bureau of the Census, Fourteenth Census: 1920, V (Agriculture), 321.

[36] Paul S. Taylor, Mexican Labor in the United States, VI, iii, 239.

[37] California, Governor Young's Fact Finding Committee, Mexicans in California, 43.

[38] Calif., SRA, Migratory, op. cit., 26.

[39] Calif., Governor Young's op. cit., 19-20.

[40] Ibid., 12.

[41] Ibid., 35.

[42] Calif., Gov. Young's, op. cit., 45.

[43] U.S., Bureau of the Census, Fifteenth Census: 1930, III, i, 2.

[44] Ibid., 233.

[45] U.S., Depart. of Labor, Bureau of Immigration, Annual Reports, fiscal years 1909-10, to 1931-32.

[46] Calif., SRA, Migratory Labor in California, 29. Compare with Table III, and Table IV, pages 11 of this study, for percentage of other nationalities in the camps.

[47] U.S. Bureau of the Census, Fifteenth Census, op. cit., 233.

[48] Calif., SRA, Migratory, op. cit., 33.

[49] Cf. ante, 26. Table VIII.

[50] Calif., SRA, Migratory, op. cit., 34. See Tables III, IV, and VII on pages 11 and 14 of this study for tables of other nationalities in the camps.

[51] Ibid., 34.

[52] Calif., Division of Immigration and Housing, Memorandum on Housing Conditions ... in California, 5.

[53] Cf. ante, 17.

CHAPTER III

THE MIGRATION TO CALIFORNIA, 1930-1940

Throughout the history of California as a state, many migrations had been sought and welcomed. From 1920 to 1930 was the period of greatest migration. During those years 2,000,000 people came to California from other states and countries.[1] This was a 60 per cent increase in population in one decade. Yet more and more newcomers were urged to come, for it was a period of business and industrial expansion. Jobs were readily available for those who came.

DEPRESSION STRIKES

With the beginning of the depression, those who had already arrived in the "Golden State" began to be concerned at the continued migration to California. They, too, were beginning to feel the depression and could foresee possible disastrous results to themselves should too many of the unemployed persons in the nation decide to move to California.

In 1931 Los Angeles seemed to be over-run by hordes of unattached, migrant men and boys. It was estimated ten thousand a month were arriving.[2] At that time it was suggested that some means be taken to stop the entrance of these men into the state, and that an investigation be made as to the source of their migration. The governor was urged to call out the state militia to halt the migrants at the state line. It had been determined that they were largely coming by freight train.

When there were added to the indigent men and boys thousands of families searching for employment, Californians became frightened and a clamor arose to stop the migration at its source.

The Federal Emergency Relief Act was passed in May, 1933. This act provided for care for the actual transient who might become stranded, but was not designed to provide for migratory workers or the homeless of the state.[3]

The earliest record of the number of transients receiving aid under the Federal Transient Service, that for December, 1933, showed 22,733 individuals cared for in California. This represented 18,697 separate cases, which indicated that

20

a large portion of those qualifying were single men, women and boys. It gave an indication of the great numbers of migrants entering the state of California at that time. The number of Federal Transient cases increased nearly every month, until a peak load of 77,118 was reached in April, 1935.[4]

On May 17, 1935, a bill was introduced in the California legislature to prevent entry into California by indigents, or those likely to become public charges.[5] This bill was backed by some of the newspapers in editorials.[6] Public protest against transients being given work relief by the government led to cessation of such relief. The Federal Transient Service issued a warning to people who might be considering migration to California that no further work relief could be given to those who entered the state after August 1, 1935.[7]

The Los Angeles Chamber of Commerce urged the use of hard-labor prison camps for vagrants as a means of discouraging indigents from coming to California, and to Los Angeles in particular.[8]

LOS ANGELES "EXTENDS HER BORDERS"

Finally, Los Angeles city policemen were sent to the various border stations, beginning on February 4, 1936, to forcibly turn back migrants, either by automobile or by freight train. This brought protests not only from officials of Arizona and other states, but from some members of the Los Angeles City Council. Such use of the police had not been authorized by the council and the legality of the action was considered questionable.[9] When the matter was referred to Los Angeles City Attorney, Ray L. Chesebro, he declared it legal for city police to be used in protection of the interests of the city even though outside the city limits.[10]

In a further attempt to make legal the use of Los Angeles policy on the borders of the state, they were deputized by the sheriffs of several of the border counties in which they were operating.

An opinion by U.S. Webb, Attorney General of California, as stated in a letter of February 18, 1936, to the Los Angeles Chamber of Commerce, declared the use of city police outside of the city limits illegal. He also stated that deputizing of police by the sheriff of a county other than the one in which the policeman legally resided was not legal.[11]

This treatment of the California-bound migrants, however, had the effect of slowing down and backing up the flood. It was estimated that it showed some effect as far east as El Paso, Texas.[12] It also brought protest from the governors of the bordering states, mayors and chiefs-of-police in the cities of the neighboring states, and a general condemnation from the press of the nation.[13]

NATION-WIDE ATTENTION ON CALIFORNIA

By 1935 the problem of migration to California had begun to attract attention all over the United States. The first of hundreds of articles which were to appear in magazines of national circulation in the six year period ending in 1941, were written, telling of the problem and in many cases offering solutions.

Publicity, however, did not slow down the migration. In 1936 the number of persons "in search of manual employment" continued to grow. It was slackened by nearly one-third in the first half of the year, perhaps due to the action of the Los Angeles police stationed along the border, but gained enough in the last half of the year to more than off-set any earlier loss.[14] September and October of that year brought the greatest influx of any like period. Over 27,000 persons in search of employment entered the state in motor vehicles in those two months.[15]

The actual number of people entering California is not known, but it was estimated that the number listed as entering by automobile "in search of manual employment" by the border check stations was only about 5 per cent of those entering the state by motor vehicle for any purpose.[16] The Los Angeles Police Department stated that 2,324,095 people entered California by automobile in 1936. Of these, nearly half entered Southern California.[17]

Again in 1937 an increase was reported in the numbers of migrants to California looking for work. More and more nation-wide attention was being given to the problem. It had now been disclosed that the Federal Transient Bureau had found that more than 12 per cent of its entire case load for 1934 and 1935 was in California.[18] It was estimated by the railway companies whose lines entered California that 97,523 transients entered California by freight train between May and November, 1937.[19]

Early 1938 continued the heavy migration, but the last half of the year showed considerable decrease. The total for the year dropped from 90,761 in 1937 to 67,664 in 1938 for out-of-state motorists in search of employment. This was a decline of more than one-fourth.[20] Publicity through such puclications as the

Saturday Evening Post reached a nationwide audience in an attempt to discourage

further migration.[21]

Migration leveled off after 1938, but at a level only slightly below that year.
As economic conditions gradually improved, the situation became less tense, but
it was more and more recognized as a national problem as well as a local problem.

Footnotes--Chapter III

[1]U.S., 76th Congress, 3d Session, House Select Committee to Investigate
the Interstate Migration of Destitute Citizens, Interstate Migration, VI, 2270.
Hereafter referred to as the Telan Committee.

[2]William T. Cross, "The Poor Migrant in California," Social Forces, XV
(March, 1937), 425.

[3]Calif., State Relief Administration, Review of Activities, 1933-1935, 169.

[4]Calif., State Emergency Relief Administration, Transients in California,
1936, 32. The case load was reported on a daily basis. The peak load for any
given month was the greatest number cared for on any day in that month.

[5]Los Angeles, Herald-Express, May 17, 1935.

[6]Ibid., May 21, 1935.

[7]Ibid., August 24, 1935.

[8]Ibid., December 11, 1935.

[9]Ibid., February 4, 1936.

[10]Ibid., February 5, 1936.

[11]Tolan Committee, Interstate Migration, VII, 2967.

[12]Edward J. Rowell, "Drought Refugee and Labor Migration to California in
1936, "U.S. Department of Labor, Monthly Labor Review, XLIII (December, 1936),
1358.

[13]"California: No Hobo Utopia," Literary Digest, CXXI (February 15, 1936), 9.

[14]Paul S. Taylor and Edward J. Rowell, "Refugee Labor Migration to California, 1937, "U.S. Department of Labor, Monthly Labor Review, XLVII (August,
1938), 242.

[15] U.S. Department of Agriculture, Farm Security Administration, "Chart showing individuals entering California in automobiles "in search of manual employment," 1935-41."

[16] Paul S. Taylor and Tom Vasey, "Drought Refugee and Labor Migration to California, June-December, 1935," U.S. Deaprtment of Labor, Monthly Labor Review, XLII (February, 1936), 318.

[17] Los Angeles Police Department, Transiency in Southern California, 1.

[18] Calif., State Emergency Relief Administration, Transients in California, 1936, 7.

[19] Los Angeles Police, Transiency, op. cit., 18.

[20] U.S. Department of Agriculture, FSA, op. cit.

[21] "No Jobs in California," Saturday Evening Post, CCXI (November 12, 1938), 18-40.

CHAPTER IV

SOURCES OF THE RECENT MIGRATION

The Bureau of Plant Quarantine of the California Department of Agriculture maintained border check stations where all incoming motor vehicles were stopped and checked to prevent entry of plants or fruits which might introduce plant diseases or pests into California. It was decided that these check stations could also check on the origin of all automobiles and on the number of occupants in cars bearing families in which the family head was in need of manual employment. This check started in June, 1935. In this way definite figures were secured as to the source of the new migration--at least of that part which entered the state by motor vehicle in search of employment. No information was available as to the numbers entering the state by rail, or of those entering the state as "tourists," but who decided to remain as residents.

It was found that nearly 20 per cent of those entering California "in need of manual employment" were returning Californians. This percentage dropped during 1936 and 1937, the peak years of the migration, but returned to that figure in 1938 and remained near that point through 1940. It was estimated by the Farm Security Administration that as much as 50 per cent of the entrants shown as coming from other states may also have been returning Californins who had been gone long enough to secure automobile licenses in other states.[1]

The drought of 1934 was believed to be a major cause of the migration, so the statistics for migrants from that section of the country most affected by the drought were kept separately. The border check stations termed Arizona, Arkansas, Colorado, Idaho, Iowa, Kansas, Minnesota, Missouri, Montana, Nebraska, Nevada, New Mexico, North Dakota, Oklahoma, South Dakota, Texas, Utah, Wisconsin, and Wyoming all as "Drought States". The true "Dust Bowl", however, consisted of only parts of five states: New Mexico, Texas, Oklahoma, Kansas and Colorado.[2]

Throughout the period during which a definite check was made on migrants entering California, the states of Oklahoma, Arizona, Texas, Arkansas and Missouri led the list in each tabulation.

WEST SOUTH-CENTRAL STATES

Leading the country in migration to California were three of the four West South-Central States: Oklahoma, Texas, and Arkansas. The fourth state in this region, Louisiana, played only a very small part in the migration at any time during the decade.

Oklahoma led all other states each year. From July 1, 1935 until the end of 1938, more than 65,000 persons from families in need of employment were listed as entering the state of California in motor vehicles bearing Oklahoma licenses.[3] This constituted 22.9 per cent of all migrants entering California during that period. There was little decrease in the total number of migrants in 1939, or in proportions for the various states.

In third place in the migration from individual states to California was Texas.[4] While Texas showed a net increase in population from 1930 to 1940 of 10.1 per cent (590,109 people)[5] and a net migration loss of only 0.3 per cent (20,131 people) from 1935 to 1940,[6] border check stations reported 29,342 persons in families from Texas in need of employment entered California between July 1, 1935 and December 31, 1938. This constituted 10.4 per cent of the migrants to California during those years.[7]

Arkansas was in fourth place in all lists of migrants to California from 1935 to 1940. Testimony before the Tolan Committee in their hearings at Oklahoma City in September, 1940, indicated that Arkansas is still greatly over-populated in relation to the resources of the state. Dr. William H. Metzler, Professor of Rural Economics at the University of Arkansas stated that 100,000 people had migrated from Arkansas each decade since 1890, and estimated that the state still had 450,000 excess farm population when compared with the United States average.[8] Arkansas gained 94,905 people between 1930 and 1940, or an increase of 5.1 per cent[9] but sustained a net migration loss of 3.9 per cent, or 75,463 persons, during the same period.[10] Of the migrants from Arkansas, 22,168 are shown to have entered California in the three and one-half years ending 1938. This made up 7.7 per cent of all migrants to California.[11]

A study of 6,655 migrant households in California who were receiving emergency grants from the Farm Security Administration in 1938 showed an even larger percentage of migrants from the West South-Central States. This area provided 4,575 families, or 68.74 per cent of the total number. Oklahoma again led with 41.64 per cent; Texas was second, with 15.67 per cent; and Arkansas was third with 10.73 per cent of the total.[12]

WEST NORTH-CENTRAL STATES

The West North-Central States, consisting of Minnesota, Iowa, Missouri, North Dakota, South Dakota, Nebraska and Kansas also furnished a large number of migrants. Of these states the only ones furnishing migrants to California in important numbers or percentage were Missouri and Kansas. Migrants from the other, more northern, states in this region went to states further north on the Pacific coast.

Missouri held fifth place in the border check station reports on migrants to California, and fourth place in the study by the Farm Security Administration in California.[13] The border check stations in California reported 18,692 Missourians, or 6.5 per cent of the total migrants for the checking period, 1935-1938. The Farm Security Administration found 7.06 per cent of the 6,655 families in their study to be from Missouri. Missouri gained 155,297 in population, or an increase of 4.3 per cent, from 1930 to 1940, but had a net migration loss for the period 1935-1940 of 85,489, or 2.3 per cent.

Kansas was in sixth place in the reports of the border check stations, but dropped to eighth rating in the group assisted by the Farm Security Administration. While Kansas showed a net loss in population of 79,971, or 4.3 per cent, from 1930 to 1940, and a net migration loss of 111,050, or 6.2 per cent, from 1935 to 1940, these people either migrated to some state other than California or were in a financial condition not requiring relief. Less than 13,000 Kansans were counted by the border check stations in California in the three and one-half years ending 1938.

MOUNTAIN STATES

Contributor of the next largest group of migrants to California were the Mountain States. Of this group, Arizona, New Mexico, and Colorado were most important.

The actual number of migrants coming from Arizona was not known. The border check stations in California showed Arizona in second place with 11.3 per cent of all migrants, or 31,907 persons, for the years 1935 to 1938. This check, however, was made by automobile license plates and not by questioning the persons involved. It was generally believed that many of those driving Arizona cars started from one of the other heavy contributing states and came as far as Arizona where they worked in the cotton picking until the end of the season. Since the cotton picking season ran through until January, February, or even March, a new automobile license would have been purchased and that group would then have been listed as coming from Arizona.[14]

Perhaps the Farm Security Administration figures showing 5.32 per cent of those receiving grants from that bureau in California in 1938 from Arizona was made nearer the correct proportion of migration originating in Arizona.

New Mexico and Colorado also contributed important numbers in the recent migration, both by border check station and Farm Security Administration reports. This was true even though both of these states increased in population during the decade more than the United States average. Indeed, New Mexico showed an increase of 25.6 per cent as compared with 21.7 per cent for California.

OTHER STATES

The only other region sending important numbers of migrants to California were the other Pacific States, Oregon and Washington. Much of the migration from these states was secondary in nature, actually originating in other states but stopping long enough to be attributed to those states. Some sources also attribute most migration from Oregon and Washington to habitual migrants.[15]

There were some cases of migration to California from practically every state in the union, as well as from Alaska, Canada, Mexico, and countries outside the continent.

PREVIOUS STATUS OF MIGRANTS

It was contended by some that the new white migrant worker in California was a dispossessed farmer who had owned his farm. An investigation of 320 cases of migrants receiving relief in the Imperial Valley of California between 1935 and

1937 showed only 5 out of 320 who reported they had ever owned any land.[16] In the Study of 6,655 Migrant Households in California in 1938 it was found that 3.7 per cent reported ownership of land at some time, while 11.8 per cent reported a non-agricultural background.[17]

A study of farm tenancy showed that the states of Oklahoma, Texas and Arkansas, three of the heaviest contributors of migrants to California, were among the states showing the highest percentage of farm tenants. In each of these states more than 60 per cent of the farmers were tenants or sharecroppers as early as 1930.[18]

These investigations indicate that a major portion of those migrants who became migratory laborers had not at any time had the security of farm ownership.

Footnotes--Chapter IV

[1] U.S. Department of Agriculture, FSA, "Chart", op. cit.

[2] Taylor and Vasey, "Drought Refugees," op. cit., 313.

[3] Tolan Committee, Interstate Migration, VII, 2973.

[4] Arizona was in second place in the migration, but was not in this group of states.

[5] U.S., Bureau of the Census, Sixteenth Census: 1940, I, 19.

[6] Ibid., II, 18.

[7] Tolan Committee, op. cit., 2973.

[8] Ibid., V, 2014-2015.

[9] U.S. Bureau of the Census, Sixteenth, op. cit., 19.

[10] Ibid., II, 18.

[11] Tolan Committee, op. cit., 2973.

[12] U.S. Department of Agriculture, FSA, A Study of 6655 Migrant Households, 1938, 14.

[13] The FSA and border check station reports were the basis for all statistics used for the West North-Central States.

[14] Paul S. Taylor and Edward J. Rowell, "Refugee Labor," op. cit., 243.

[15] Edward J. Rowell, "Drought Refugee and Labor Migration to California in 1936," U.S. Department of Labor, Monthly Labor Review, XLIII (December, 1936), 1360.

[16] Paul S. Taylor and Edward J. Rowell, "Refugee Labor Migration, 1937", U.S. Department of Labor, Monthly Labor Review, XLVII (August, 1938), 245-256.

[17] U.S. Department of Agriculture, FSA, Study of 6655 Migrant Households, 1938, 59.

[18] U.S., National Resources Committee, Farm Tenancy, 96.

CHAPTER V

DIRECT AND CONTRIBUTING CAUSES OF THE MIGRATION

OF THE 1930's

There were many reasons for the migration of large numbers of people from their former place of residence in the 1930's. Some of these causes were not immediate, but went back into the history of the development of the United States, and particularly of the Great Plains.

Three waves of migration followed one upon another in the development of the United States. The first wave was made up of Indian traders and trappers. They were the first white men to advance upon the new regions to the west. Following more or less closely on their heels came the cattlemen, who were the first settlers of the new west, for "Beef and pork and mutton were the only crops in that land without roads which could take themselves to market."[1]

The third wave of migration was that of the farmers with their plows, constantly forcing the cattle further and further to the west.

Between 1865 and 1885 the Great Plains were filled with pioneers. Foreign capital had become interested and there were numerous English and German cattle ranches there.

THE HOMESTEAD ACT

The Homestead Act of 1862 brought the plow to the plains. This act made available to anyone who cared to settle on it, 160 acres of land. By 1890 the population of the Dakotas had grown to 510,000. The railroads had done their part in recruiting settlers for the plains, for by so doing they were building business for their new system of transportation which passed through this region.

This was the region of the short grass, indicating that it was a region of limited rainfall in normal years, yet that did not seem to bother the new settler. As the region became more fully settled it was found that 160 acres was not sufficient to provide a living for a family. In 1909 the Homestead Act was altered to increase the acreage from 160 to 320 in a homestead.[2]

In 1912 the period of residence for "proving up" on a homestead was reduced from five years to three, as an added inducement to attract new settlers. Finally in 1916 the homestead acreage was increased to 640 acres (a full section) of grazing land in a further attempt to provide new homes for settlers in the west.[3]

All remaining public grasslands were withdrawn from entry for homesteading in 1934, at the time large-scale soil reclamation was started, in order to prevent further unnecessary erosion.

SOIL EROSION

By 1885 the range land was overstocked by from two to three times the number of cattle it could normally carry. An unusually severe winter in 1886-1887 cost the cattlemen millions of dollars in cattle losses. In 1893 the southwest experienced the same fate.

As time showed that the range was over-cattled, sheepmen began to come upon the scene. This brought about the cattlemen-sheepmen feuds which provided the theme for numerous stories of the 1890's. Sheep will graze on grass that is too short for cattle to eat, but they eat the grass below the growing bud in doing so and in this way kill the grass. When there is not sufficient grass they will feed upon the willows and other brush, and still further deplete the soil covering. Sheep have small, sharp hoofs, which cut up wet ground, even though it is covered with sod. Thus, the coming of the sheep was the beginning of the end for the range land. Soil that is cut up and denuded soon erodes, both by rain and by wind.[4]

An illustration of how sheep can cause destruction of the land is that of the Navajo Indian Reservation in Arizona and New Mexico. The Navajos were preceded by the Pueblo Indians who were good farmers. When the Navajos came to the reservation in 1868 they brought their cattle and sheep. The sheep were increased greatly in numbers, as the Navajos themselves increased from 8,000 in 1868 to 45,000 in 1935, and by 1935 the grass was gone. The Navajos retreated into the uplands leaving great arroyos twenty and thirty feet deep across the former pastureland. In 1934 the soil conservation experts began working in an attempt to reclaim this land.[5]

Another cause of erosion was the transfer of grazing land to cultivated drop-
land during and following World War I. The Department of Agriculture encouraged
dry farming on the plains, and the three wet years of 1914, 1915 and 1916 further
encouraged this trend on the part of those who were already in that region. The
World War, with its high wheat prices, caused thousands upon thousands of acres
of sod to be broken and planted to wheat. As this first land began to be depleted,
additional land was broken in sections of even less rainfall. Some of it was not
broken until from 1928 to 1931.[6]

The term "Great Plains" could be misleading, giving the impression of a vast
level region. That was not true, however, as much of the area is rolling, or hilly.
It was partly due to this rolling characteristic that water erosion was as great a
problem as it came to be. The farmers of the region followed the old system of
planting row crops in straight rows without regard to the lay of the land. Running
ridges and ditches up and down the slope of the land started rapid erosion. After
a few years gullies began to develop, or sometimes even one extremely heavy rain
might practically ruin a newly plowed field.

Types of soil also played a part in erosion. Much of the region was made up
of light, somewhat sandy, soils which washed or blew easily. If there was a clay
topsoil, in many cases that soon eroded in small ditches down to a lighter soil which
then rapidly wore away and destroyed the land.

With the land being rapidly depleted or eroded it followed that any other unusual
condition would have greater than normal effect upon the residents of the region.
The years 1930 to 1940 brought a number of unusual circumstances to this area.

DEPRESSION

The depression which lasted more or less throughout the decade 1930 to 1940
was commonly charged to the stock market crash of October, 1929. The depression
for the farmer, however, had started prior to that[7] with falling prices which caused
him concern as to how he could meet the debts he had incurred during the boom years
of 1916 to 1921.[8] At that time a large number of the farmers had purchased additional land at inflated prices, mortgaging their original holdings to do so, or had
mortgaged their land for large sums to build good homes and outbuildings and for
purchase of other equipment. Falling prices, even with normal crop returns,

made it difficult for these men to meet their obligations and maintain their families.

With the general depression that followed the crash in the fall of 1929, crop values dropped lower and lower, and combined with decreasing rainfall cut farm income to a point where it showed a net loss in many cases.

As farm mortgage payments became delinquent, foreclosures started. Over 1,500,000 farms, constituting more than one-fourth of all farms in the United States, were lost between 1930 and 1939 through inability to meet payments on the mortgage, or inability to pay the taxes on the land.[9] Many of the mortgages were held by large insurance companies who had been investing large amounts of money in farm mortgages since 1920. While in many cases the insurance company improved the property acquired, the former owner became a tenant and usually moved to another farm. Other mortgages were held by individuals and by banks. Many of the individuals and banks took over the farms they acquired and operated them as part of large units, as they could earn greater returns on their investments in that way.[10]

Those farmers who did not have mortgages on their land found it difficult to meet even the taxes on their property. In some areas it was reported to the Tolan Committee that counties acquired large sections of land because of delinquent taxes.[11]

DROUGHT

The drought was believed by the public to be the principal cause of migration. It was also given by the migrants themselves, as a chief cause. Undoubtedly the drought was a direct and immediate reason for migration, but it was tied up with the other factors which have been given.

While the drought of 1934 was the immediate cause of creation of the "Dust bowl" which was widely publicized, 1934 was not the first year of this unprecedented condition.

The year 1929 began a new period of drought in the west central section of the United States. This was the first such period after the last sod-breaking.[12] The ground was plowed and loose and a poor crop was harvested. The year 1930 was again dry, with a resulting poor crop in much of the region. There was still deficient rainfall in 1931, but a large wheat crop was harvested in the Southern Great Plains. Increased moisture fell in 1932, but it was still below normal in much of the region. The year 1933 was no better than 1931.[13]

Then came 1934--the year of the "Great Drought." The land had been abnormally dry for several years, and now added to the drought were hot, dry winds which whipped and swirled the dust and sand into the air, creating the almost unbelievable dust storms. The dust was carried for hundreds of miles, causing dust storms in cities far removed from the source of the dust. Locally, the dust and sand were piled into dunes rising twenty and thirty feet high. Fences became walls of dust and sand. Buildings and roads were buried in great drifts, as with snow after a blizzard. All top soil was blown away to a depth of several inches in many places. Sod land was ruined by the drifting dirt which covered and skilled the grass.[14]

The drought of 1934 reached far beyond the true "Dust Bowl" region, and seriously affected most of the Middle West. In some places, corn planted in the spring was found to be unsprouted in the ground in the fall. Weeds did not even start by the side of the road, and the old growth was covered by blown dust. Mud rains were experienced in some places when a light shower would fall while a dust storm was in progress.[15]

A drought of this extent would have had serious results had it been of only one year's duration and in otherwise normal times, but coming in the midst of a general economic depression and following several years of below-normal rainfall, it was disastrous. Streams of victims began to pour out of the region, and many of them headed west toward California.[16]

But 1934 was still not the end of the drought period. It continued on through the decade. It was reported that in one Kansas high plains county of above-average fertility, only 28 per cent of the wheat acreage planted was harvested during an eight-year period, and that the average yield per acre of that harvested was only four bushels per acre. This was also accompanied by a feed crop failure several of the years.[17]

In some sections there was no weed growth during the eight-year period, 1933-1940. As much as 40 per cent of the population left some areas (not allowing for the normal population increase of 6 to 10 per cent). School enrollment in some counties dropped to an average of less than five pupils per school, because of the departure of the residents.[18]

It was estimated by Edwin R. Henson, Coordinator for the United States

Department of Agriculture at Amarillo, Texas, in 1940, that from 6,000,000 to 8,000,000 acres of land in the Southern Great Plains needed regrassing, including land then under cultivation as well as denuded range lands.[19]

Drought states, such as Nebraska, in which there were some irrigated sections reported that the irrigated areas held their own in population in spite of some shortage of irrigation water due to the lack of snow and rain in the mountain watershed area, while some dry-farming counties in the same state lost one family in four.[20]

MECHANIZED AGRICULTURE

While earlier reports had indicated a general belief on the part of the migrants that they had been "blown out" or "dusted out" by the drought, in 1937 an occasional report saying "tractored out" was heard. This led to investigation as to the increase of the use of tractors or mechanized farming in the various parts of the country, and the effect of the coming of the tractor on the former tenant and farm laborer.[21]

An article in the Semi-weekly Farm News of Dallas, Texas, under the date of January 19, 1937, presented the situation in Hall County in western Texas. It stated that there were numerous large landowners in that county, each of whom had from ten to twenty tenant farmers. Some of these tenants had resided on the same farm for as long as eighteen years. In 1937, 420 of these tenants were being forced from the farm through purchase of tractors by the landowner. This meant displacement of 2,100 people. The owner planned to hire a man to operate a tractor at a wage of $1.25 per day. He would also be able to collect the full amount of money paid for retirement of land from production under the Agricultural Adjustments Administration program which was formerly shared with the tenant.[22]

The government crop-adjustment money was the one remaining cash resource to many landowners. It was declared by many of those appearing before the Tolan Committee to be the means by which the owner was able to purchase a tractor. The landowner, who was in many cases having difficulty in meeting payments on his land, seized the opportunity to try to get ahead.

Paul S. Taylor, in testimony before the United States Senate Special Committee to Investigate Unemployment and Relief on March 14, 1938, said that one cotton planter in the Mississippi Delta purchased twenty-two tractors which displaced 130 of his former 160 sharecropper families. He retained the other thirty families to have an available supply of day labor.[23] This same case is cited in several articles written during the period, but Mr. Taylor testified that he secured the information directly from the planter, Mr. J. H. Aldridge of Greenville, Mississippi.

In Southwestern Texas there was, between 1931 and 1938, an increase of 165 per cent in number of tractors used. The greatest increase came after 1935, as of 98,966 tractors in Texas in 1938, more than 50,000 were purchased after 1935. It was estimated by Edwin R. Henson of the United States Department of Agriculture that from one to three families were displaced by each tractor.[24]

One Oklahoma banker, oil operator and farmer stated that displacement of farmers by tractors occurred not only directly, but indirectly. The great increase in the use of tractors, trucks, and automobiles nearly eliminated the production of feed and forage crops and increased by a like amount the acreage devoted to production of human food. This increase in the production of food crops was a factor in forcing down the price of the crops.[25]

Mechanization first struck the Wheat Belt, where it eliminated the migratory wheat harvest hand. Next came the Cotton Belt, where mechanization was still advancing rapidly in the 1930's. From 1930 to 1937 the sale of farm tractors increased 50 per cent throughout the United States, but in the cotton states the increase was 90 per cent. Oklahoma, Texas, and Arkansas were three of the states most affected by this increased sale of tractors. Economists concluded that if the trend continued a majority of the 1,800,000 tenants in the South would be added to the other jobless and landless, many of whom became migrants.[26]

The most recent crop belt to be widely mechanized was the Corn Belt. It was estimated that 6 per cent of Iowa's farm families were pushed off the land by tractors between 1937 and 1940.[27] One Iowa farmer who expanded his operations from 200 acres in 1937 to 1,000 acres in 1940, said the farmers he displaced with his tractors moved into southern Iowa where the land is poorer. There, by means of their superior equipment and methods, they displaced other farmers who went to the Ozarks of Missouri and Arkansas to displace other tenants who moved out as migrants--probably on the trail to the west and California.[28] An increase of 110.7 per cent in the use of tractors was recorded in the Corn Belt between 1930 and 1940.[29]

Throughout the central part of the United States the same situation prevailed. Whether it be Texas, Oklahoma, Arkansas, or Iowa, the tractor was making rapid inroads and displacing more and more of the former residents of the land.

OTHER FACTORS

Many other reasons were given for the displacement of those who were classed as migrants. E. H. Aicher, Chief of the Institutional Adjustments Division of the Soil Conservation Service at Lincoln, Nebraska, gave the following factors in the instability and movement of the rural population from the Northern Plains States:

First, the great variance in the soils and climate in the region. This ranged from rich bottom land to dry sand and clay, and from areas of ample normal rainfall to regions in which the usual rainfall would not produce a cultivated crop but might maintain the native sod if not pastured too closely.

Second, the method of settlement made for uneconomic use of the land. The homestead system and the "high-pressure" land companies both settled the pioneer on any land in the region without regard to its climate or soil.

Third, the farmers of the region were greatly over-capitalized following the boom years of 1916-1921. With abundant crops and high prices the farmer attempted to expand his holdings by mortgaging his land at an inflated value to purchase other land for which he was paying a similarly inflated price. Others mortgaged the land to build fine homes and other improvements, or for additional farm equipment. This saddled the farmer with a debt too great for even "normal" times.

Fourth, the over-expansion of public facilities, through extension of the township system, the one-room school, and similar small-unit government expenditures which raised the tax level unduly high.

Fifth, the expansion of public and private credit.[30]

Sixth, the introduction of power machinery in agricultural operations. This increased the expense of farming and made necessary the expansion of operations in order to make a profit.

Seventh, the insecurity of tenure. Farms in the area are customarily rented on verbal agreement for one year at a time.

Eighth, severe climatic reverses. Subnormal rainfall throughout the region after 1928.[31]

Ninth, use of a type of farming adapted to regions of greater rainfall instead of attempting to take advantage of what rainfall was available normally.[32]

Governor Leon C. Phillips of the state of Oklahoma added to the reasons already given some which applied in that state, and some which may have applied elsewhere as well. He placed discriminatory freight rates for Oklahoma as a prime factor in the displacement. This factor was held to be chiefly responsible for the decline of mining operations and partly for the decline in oil production. Coal mining reached its peak in Oklahoma in 1920, while there were vast fields which were never developed and the mining of the fields already opened dropped to one-third of the 1920 level. Zinc mining was cut in half from 1930 to 1939. Zinc smelting and glass making also declined. Decline in industry caused an agricultural displacement through loss of local markets for food products.

Governor Phillips charged the national policy of crop curtailment (which reduced cultivation of cash by one-third in Oklahoma) with stimulating owner-farming which displaced many of the tenants. He also blamed the loss of foreign markets for corn, cotton and wheat for much of the migration.[33]

Newspaper advertisements in Texas and Oklahoma papers describing wonderful opportunities for farm labor in California have been "rumored" and reported in many unidentified "hearsay" stories, but none have even been produced.[34]

Lack of work was given by many of the migrants as the reason for leaving their former place of residence. That was of course true, but that lack of work could be traced in most cases to one of the other factors, or to a combination of them.

Health was presented as the reason for migrating to California by 7.47 per cent of those migrants studied by the Farm Security Administration,[35] while more than 20 per cent of those on Transient Relief in California in 1935 gave reasons of health for migrating.[36] The state of health may also have been influenced by some of the other factors listed.

High relief payments were advanced by some sources as a great influence in directing migration to California. This factor was included in the reasons given by the California State Chamber of Commerce. However, the residence laws which required residence in the state for a full year before receiving work relief, or three years before receiving relief as an unemployable, were a great deterrent in that factor.

Additional reasons given by the California Chamber of Commerce for the migrants having left their placed of origin included high birth rates, inadequate local relief, and increased mobility of the population due to development of the automobile and good roads. Other factors, according to the same source, which attracted the migrant to California included higher wage rates,[37] development of the cotton industry on a large scale following 1932, and labor recruiting by Arizona cotton growers in Texas, Oklahoma, and Arkansas by means of Handbills, newspaper advertisements, travel agents and other means.[38]

There were perhaps other minor factors in displacement of the migrants, but they would in most cases be connected very closely with factors already given.

Footnotes--Chapter V

[1]"The Grasslands," Fortune, November, 1935, 61.

[2]William Spry, "Homestead and Exemption Laws," Encyclopedia Brittanica, 14th edition, XI, 705.

[3]Loc. cit.

[4]"The Grasslands," Fortune, November, 1935, 66.

[5]Ibid., 190.

[6]Tolan Committee, op. cit., 1762-1763. Report of Edwin R. Henson, Coordinator, United States Department of Agriculture, Amarillo, Texas.

[7]Charles A. and Mary R. Beard, A Basic History of the United States, 452.

[8]Tolan Committee, op. cit., IV, 1611-1617.

[9]H. Hendricks, "Farmers Without Farms," The Atlantic Monthly, CLXVI (October, 1940), 461.

[10]Tolan Committee, op. cit., V, 2082-2086.

[11]This condition was reported in testimony from Colorado, Oklahoma, Nebraska, and other states.

[12] Cf. ante, 52.

[13] Tolan Committee, op. cit., V, 1762.

[14] Ibid., 1763.

[15] This condition was actually witnessed by the writer.

[16] Taylor and Vasey, "Drought Refugee", op. cit., 312.

[17] Tolan Com., op. cit., V, 1764.

[18] Ibid., 1765-1766.

[19] Ibid., 1764.

[20] Ibid., IV, 1350.

[21] Taylor and Rowell, "Refugee Labor ..." op. cit., 243.

[22] U.S., 75th Congress, 3d Session, Senate Special Committee to Investigate Unemployment and Relief, Extract from Hearings, exhibit 4, 1610 f.

[23] Ibid., 1161. Statement of Paul S. Taylor.

[24] Tolan Committee, op. cit., V, 1814.

[25] Ibid., 2082.

[26] "I Wonder Where We Can Go Now," Fortune, XIX, (April, 1939), 112.

[27] H. Hendricks, "Farmers Without Farms," The Atlantic Monthly, CLXVI (October, 1940), 461.

[28] Tolan Com., op. cit., VIII, 3256.

[29] Ibid., X, 4064.

[30] Cf. ante, Third, this page. These two points are closely allied.

[31] Cf. ante, 54 ff.

[32] Tolan Com., op. cit., IV, 1611-17.

[33] Ibid., V, 2033-41.

[34] "Flee Dustbowl for California," Business Week, July 3, 1937, 36; "The Okies--A National Problem," Business Week, February 10, 1940, 17.

[35] U.S., Department of Agriculture, Farm Security Administration, A Study of 6655 Migrant Households, 1938, 31.

[36] Tolan Committee, op. cit., VII, 2768.

[37] The day wage rate in California for farm labor was more than twice that in any of the states which were sources of great migration to California. Piece rates, such as for cotton picking, were about 50 per cent higher in California.

[38] Tolan Committee, op. cit., VII, 2763-8.

CHAPTER VI

THE EFFECTS OF THE RECENT MIGRATION TO CALIFORNIA

Just as important were the widespread and diverse effects of the migration of the 1930's on California. One source might consider that the results were purely economic, while another could be interested in simply the social effects. Still a third source would have in mind only the political situation in California. Each of these was important, and each must be considered in order to complete the picture.

ECONOMIC AND SOCIAL EFFECTS

As has been noted earlier, the types of agriculture carried on in California required great amounts of labor for short seasons. This was a factor in developing large industrialized ranches, or "Factories in the Field," as Carey McWilliams has so aptly termed them in his book of that title.[1] Dr. Paul S. Taylor of the University of California stated that of all the large-scale farms in the United States, more than one-third are in California. In the Pacific States the large farms (those which employ ten or more laborers) constitute less than 1 per cent of the farms, but employ about one-third of all paid farm laborers in that region.[2]

The number of agricultural laborers actually needed at any one time has never been very accurately determined. It has been known, however, that the maximum number is required in September. Harrison S. Robinson of the California State Chamber of Commerce estimated a peak of 144,720 workers were needed in September, and this dropped to a low of 48,173 laborers in March. An extreme was shown in Sonoma County. There, 8,840 agricultural laborers were required to care for the crops in September, whereas only 500 were needed in November.[3] A survey conducted by the State Emergency Relief Administration in 1935 showed a maximum of 198,349 workers needed throughout the state in September. This dropped to a minimum of 46,448 in December and January.

This survey showed that the requirements had risen to 61,316 laborers by March.[4] Whether this was the number of workers actually needed to perform the necessary labor in the various months, or the number of workers which the growers would like to have available, was not made entirely clear.

The actual number of available workers at any given time was impossible to ascertain. Being a migrant group, and not having secured employment, or attempted to do so, through the medium of an agency, only estimates were possible. These estimates varied from a low of 150,000 to a high of 350,000 in the opinions of various people. Research by Dr. H. Gregory Silvermaster of the State Relief Administration showed 142 workers for every 100 jobs in agriculture during the first seven months of 1934. On that basis, it was estimated that after 1935 there were from two to three workers available for every job in California agriculture.[5]

In spite of this tremendous source of labor for agriculture, growers still complained of a shortage of labor at times. Part of any possible shortage seemed to be due to lack of any organized system of labor placement in California. Although the California State Employment Service offered its services to agricultural laborers, and to the growers, neither group partonized the service to any great extent.

The growers, through their organization, the Associated Farmers, charged that the employment service would not furnish workers in sufficient numbers, or quickly enough when needed. The Associated Farmers also stated that it was the policy of the State Employment Service to follow a federal regulation under the Wagner-Peyser Act, forbidding referral of any worker to a job where there was a labor dispute in progress. It was claimed that a "communist" agitator would enter the employment office and state that a wage dispute was in progress at some farm which was in great need of workers to save a perishable crop, thus preventing referral of workers and resulting in crop spoilage. Kern County was cited as an example. It was declared that eighty such cases occurred in that one county in 1939.[6]

The workers claimed that the California State Employment Service was a tool of the organized growers, and combined with them to send too many workers to a job, in this way attempting to force wages to a lower level.

In 1940, the State Employment Service opened agricultural labor information offices, one at Indio, another near Bakersfield, and a third on the west side of the Pacheco Pass, in an attempt to help cut the travel of the migrants and to guide them to jobs.[7]

Private labor contractors still continued to operate extensively throughout California, and the migratory families continued to travel great distances from one job to another, often needlessly. It was found that the average migrant family in California traveled 516 miles between jobs during the year, and that 28 per cent of these families traveled more than 1,000 miles each. Some families traveled as much as 3,000 miles a year in search of work.[8]

Investigation by the United States Department of Labor showed that the average migrant family had an annual cash income of only $250 to $450 a year.[9] Out of this amount, nearly half was required for expense on the automobile which furnished transportation from job to job. This low level of income in many cases forced the family to seek public assistance at some time during the year.

Relief, or public assistance, was offered by numerous private organizations in California, as well as by the county, state and federal government agencies. The county, state and private assistance had existed to some extent over a period of many years. Many new agencies, however, were established, and to these were added the federal agencies created so freely after 1933.

The Federal Emergency Relief Act of 1933 provided for grants to the individual states to aid them in meeting the costs of providing for persons in need. The benefits from these funds were required to be made available to all in need, regardless of whether they be classed as residents, transients, or homeless.[10] As the emergency continued, and a more extensive relief program was developed, the homeless or transient person found himself in a serious situation.

In an attempt to make the burden on the local taxpayers as light as possible the state and county agencies set up rigid requirements of residence which must be met before assistance could be given to the needy. California laws provided for assistance to families, or individuals, with no employable person, through the County Departments of Charities, while families in which there was an employable person, were cared for by the State Relief Administration until such time as the employable person could be assigned to the Works Progress Administration for work relief, or secured private employment. For a short period the State also conducted a program of work relief, but this was discontinued with the development of the WPA program.

When the residence requirements were applied to those in need of assistance it was found that many could not qualify for any relief from the local agencies. When no other public agency could care for these people, they were referred to one of the so-called private agencies, if the emergency seemed great, but the number of cases overtaxed the resources of the private agencies.[11]

There were numerous indications that the recent migrants to California added materially to the numbers of persons receiving aid through the State Relief Administration and perhaps from the other local agencies as well, both directly and indirectly.

A report by H. Dewey Anderson, Administrator of the State Relief Administration (SRA) in California in February, 1939, gave statistics which showed some of the effects of the migration. Of the persons on SRA relief rolls on February 11, 1939, 34.1 per cent had entered the state of California during the period 1930 to 1939, while 21.4 per cent had arrived in the period 1935 to 1939. This indicated something of the inability of recent migrants to secure adequate employment after arriving in California, which had a direct effect on taxes and relief in the state.[12]

Another supposed influence of the migration on taxes and relief although indirect, was the fact that persons classed as "Mexican" constituted 25.2 per cent of all SRA relief recipients on February 11, 1939, while the census of 1930 listed only 6.5 per cent of the residents of California at that time as "Mexican" and the percentage had decreased since 1930. As the Mexican was an important source of migratory agricultural labor in California, this seemed to indicate that many Mexicans were displaced by the new migrants, and being unable to find other work were thrown on relief. By comparing these figures with relief figures for 1908, however, it appeared merely a continuation of an old situation.[13]

There were several attempts at economic rehabilitation of the California migrants. One of the first of these was at Salinas.

In 1933, just east of Salinas, a "shanty-town" for 200 people was started. It was originally labeled "Little Oklahoma," by the residents of Salinas, because many of the settlers were from Oklahoma, and the others were from other west central states. These people bought small plots of ground (50 by 120 feet) for two hundred dollars. They paid fifty dollars down and were given four years to pay the balance. There were even a few tiny lots 50 feet square, and these were purchased for a total price of fifty dollars. Through the industry of these individuals they made their way up in the world. By 1940 many of the original settlers were "landlords" in the thriving little community which was then called "East Salinas". This group of people largely built their own homes, starting with a very small house and adding to it as they could. They cultivated their own ground, and secured part-time work within driving distance from their new homes. It was an example of what could be done.[14]

Another experiment of resettling the migrants on the land in California was carried out by Social Adjustments, Incorporated. This agency was established to set up non-relief families on one acre of ground at a rent equal to 6 per cent interest on the bank appraisal of re-possessed property for a period of five years. The average rental was about $2.50 per month. At the end of the five-year period the renter could buy the land on low-term payments over a period of five or ten years. The agency supplied the seeds and a hoe. The contract provided that within the first year the renter must complete a hand-made shelter, usually of adobe, on the land. Areas were selected in which part-time employment could be secured by the settlers, and where fertile soil and adequate water supply were available. This followed the plan of "Shore Acres," which had been established near Los Angeles in 1933, by the Security-First National Bank of Los Angeles. In the latter project, 600 families successfully established themselves.[15]

The largest banking houses in California, Bank of America and the Security First National Bank of Los Angeles, as well as the Capitol National Bank of Sacramento, cooperated with the "Social Adjustments" plan.[16]

The appearance of John Steinbeck's Pulitzer Prize novel, Grapes of Wrath, in 1939 created a furor throughout the country, and especially in California. Based on the migration from Oklahoma to California after 1935, and on the social and economic condition of the migrant farm laborer in California, it was frequently compared with the Uncle Tom's Cabin of an earlier day.[17] While Grapes of Wrath was only a novel, and many of its situations were far from accurate, at least much of the interest in the migrant problem and in its

47

social effects can be traced to that book.

Wheeler, Mayo, editor of the Sequoyah County Times of Salislaw, Oklahoma (original home of the family chronicled in Grapes of Wrath) denied that the picture of that section of Oklahoma as portrayed in the book was true in any sense. He stated before the Tolan Committee that at the time the novel was written there were not more than ten tractors in that county, but that perhaps Steinbeck gave the farmers there new ideas on farming, as there was an increase to about sixty tractors in use in the county in 1940. Sequoyah County gained four thousand in population between 1930 and 1940.[18]

A "battle of words" over Grapes of Wrath was waged through the medium of Forum magazine between Frank J. Taylor and Carey McWilliams. Taylor attempted to give the facts behind some of the stories in Grapes of Wrath. He did not deny that conditions were bad for many of the migrants, but thought an unfair picture had been given of California authorities and relief conditions. McWilliams charged that Taylor was a publicist for the California growers and stated that Grapes of Wrath presented the best idea of economic and social conditions in California's large-scale farming region of anything written.[19] Replies were made by readers to the articles written by Taylor and McWilliams, under the title "Wrath on Both Sides".[20]

The "Hooverville" shack-town at Bakersfield had been given publicity before the writing of Grapes of Wrath.[21] This community of shacks made of tin oil cans, burlap, cardboard and rags was located just across the street from the local Chamber of Commerce. It was only one of many such communities, not only in California, but in other states as well. Pictures in the report of the President's Committee on Farm Tenancy show that many of the migrants to California had come from housing as bad as that they found in California, and that many others remained in the shelters which were left behind.[22] The "Hooverville" in Bakersfield was on low ground where it was subject to flood, and was finally moved through the efforts of the health authorities. Such shack towns could be found close to every city and town in the San Joaquin Valley, the section employing the largest number of migrants.[23]

Not only were there such slum conditions in the cities and villages, but many camps of unbelievable filth and squalor were to be found here and there throughout the agricultural regions of California. In the winter and early spring many of these squatter camps were completely mired down.[24]

Many camps were provided by the growers. These were subject to inspection by the State Division of Immigration and Housing, and were rated Good, Fair, or Bad. The report for 1940 showed that in the six southern San Joaquin Valley counties, out of 591 camps 222 were "Bad" and only 69 were rated "Good".[25] This coupled with the statement of the Associated Farmers that at their insistence $3,000,000 was spent by their members on new or improved camp facilities in the years 1937-1938, gave some indication of earlier grower camp conditions.[26]

The Federal agency which played a greater part than did any other in the economic (and perhaps social) adjustment of the migrants in California, was the Farm Security Administration. An attempt was made to care for as many as a half-million migrants on the Pacific coast through this source.[27]

The Farm Security Administration had its beginning as the Resettlement Administration under an Executive Order of the President of the United States, in 1934. The farm labor program of this agency had its beginning in California. Both praise and condemnation were showered upon the FSA, as it was known, for the program it carried on. Sometimes it was both praised and condemned by the same people for different parts of its work.

The program of the FSA included permanent, seasonal and mobile camps for farm laborers, laborers' homes for permanent occupancy, part-time farm corporations, full time farm corporations, relief through emergency grants, and subsidies to the Agricultural Workers' Health and Medical Association.[28]

The farm labor camp program was generally praised by all groups. The program started in 1935 with the construction of two camps, one at Arvin in Kern County, and the other at Marysville in Yuba County. Each of these camps had a capacity of ninety-six families. At the close of 1939 there were thirteen permanent camps in use, as well as two mobile camps which were being tried out. An addition of four permanent and two mobile camps in 1940 gave a total capacity of 5,100 family units. Each unit served an average of at least two different families during a year. Since the families averaged between four and five persons each, that meant that the program was serving about 45,000 persons at the close of 1940.[29]

The permanent camps either provided wooden platforms on which migrants could ptich their tents, or simple one-room shelters. A sanitary building, containing toilets, shower baths, and laundry tubs was provided for each forty or fifty families. Many of the camps maintained a children's clinic and nursery, with a resident nurse in charge; an isolation ward for persons with contagious diseases; provision for self-repair work on automobiles, and other facilities.[30]

The mobile camps were developed to provide for workers in regions in which the labor season was particularly short. Portable tent platforms which could be moved by truck, a first-aid and clinic trailer, a shower-bath trailer, and a laundry unit were provided.[31]

The farm laborers' homes were developed because of the tendency of many of the migrants to stay within a small area throughout the year, and the desire to try to help them to rehabilitate themselves. The first unit was built at the Arvin camp site in 1937. Twenty three-room homes with plumbing and electric lights were provided for a rental charge of $8.20 per month, including utilities. To be eligible to rent one of these homes, the family must have had a work experience of not less than one year in the community and an income between four hundred and one thousand dollars per year. By the end of 1940 there were 508 such homes provided in California by the FSA.[32]

The project of the Farm Security Administration which caused more opposition than any other was that of the Farm Corporations--or cooperative farms. It was commonly charged that an attempt was being made to "socialize" America, with this as the beginning.[33]

The first of the farm corporations in California was the Mineral King farm at Visalia. This was incorporated in 1937, but did not start actual operation until 1939. Ten families participated in the farming of the 530 acre farm the first year, receiving a $5,000 loan from the FSA to finance their operations. The FSA reported that the income of the members of this cooperative averaged about $800 for the first year--nearly twice their former earnings. It was estimated that with full development the income per family would rise to about $1,500 annually.[34] They then took in three other families and secured an additional loan from the FSA with which to build new homes.[35]

The Farm Security Administration grant program was developed in 1938 to care for agricultural families stranded in California who could not meet the residence requirements of the State Relief Administration. This program was attacked by California pressure groups who charged that it multiplied California's relief problem by inducing migrants to come to California and enabling them to remain until they were able to quality for relief under the State Relief Administration requirements.[36]

Rehabilitation loans were made to thousands of farmers, some of whom were migrants, by the Farm Security Administration. These loans were made only to farmers who could not get loans elsewhere for purchase of seed, tools, livestock, and other necessary equipment. Tenant purchase loans were also made to enable tenants, sharecroppers and laborers to buy farms of their own. Several hundred thousand loans were made at the sources of migration, as well, in an attempt to prevent further migration. A plan was set up for each family, to try to help them to make the best use of their money. Many of these loans were paid off in full in advance of the date due.[37]

Slum housing conditions coupled with poor food produced extremely bad health conditions among the migrants. Dysentery was prevalent in many of the camps that lacked means of proper sanitation. Malaria was common, particularly in the ditch-side squatter camps. Epidemics of typhoid fever, small pox, scarlet fever and other communicable diseases frequently started in the camps and spread to the rest of the community.[38] Yet it was often difficult to get the migrants to submit to vaccination and other health measures.[39]

Affecting even greater numbers than did the communicable diseases was sickness due to malnutrition. Milk was often almost completely lacking in the diet of all members of the family--even in that of the children.[40]

Because of the tremendous health problems and lack of other facilities to meet them, the Farm Security Administration financed the organization of the Agricultural Workers' Health and Medical Association in March, 1938. Dr. R. C. Williams, a Farm Security Administration physician was instrumental in setting up this organization. Representatives of the State Medical Association, the State Department of Public Health, and the FSA served as a board of directors. Medical service was limited to agricultural workers who had resided in California for less than one year. Provision was made for home and office care, hospitalization, necessary drugs and medication, emergency dental care, and special diets. Clinics were served by a panel of doctors (limited to Doctors of Medicine) and nurses who volunteered to serve. Because of the great numbers of cases in which malnutrition was the reason for sickness, doctors on the clinic panels were given the privilege of issuing grocery orders for the patients.[41]

A survey by the State Department of Health of 1,000 migrant school children in California in 1936-1937, showed medical and hygienic defects in 23 per cent more than average for the number of children. While 27 per cent had nutritional defects, nearly 16 per cent had no provision for milk in their diets.[42] Moving from place to place from three to nine or more times during the year, coupled with illness, caused children of the migrants to lose much time in school. Tests given in Tulare County showed that the mental ability of the migrant children was about average. The average migrant child, however, was retarded one year in grade placement, due to time lost because of frequent absences when moving from one place to another or because of health problems.[43] The Merced schools reported that migrant children in their schools were retarded from two to four years. Part of this was due to time lost in moving, and in staying out of school to work, as well as because of health.[44]

Irregular attendance is a problem in any school district, but even worse than the usual irregularity due to illness was the sudden influx of large numbers of children due to changing crop labor demands. Then, when the crop was finished, large numbers of children would as suddenly leave. It was also quite unpredictable as to how many of the migrant families would decide to stay in some community.

In Porterville, each year from 1938 to 1940, three additional teachers had to be employed after school opened due to unpredicted increased enrollments. A survey of the Porterville elementary schools on February 19, 1940, showed that of 1,960 children in school on that date, 718 came from migrant families who had entered California during the decade. This was more than 36 per cent of the total enrollment.[45]

The Merced schools showed a 20 per cent increase in elementary school enrollment from 1935-1940, and attributed about half of the increase of migrants from the Dust Bowl.[46]

A survey of the Southwest District of the Kern County schools gave an indication of the effect of the migration of the decade on that area. Of 2,312 pupils in that district, 982 were born in Oklahoma, 723 in California, 224 in Texas, 124 in Arkansas, 46 in Missouri, and the rest in thirty-one other states and two foreign countries.[47]

POLITICAL EFFECT

During the decade of the 1930's California changed from a predominately Republican to an overwhelmingly Democratic state. This change cannot all be credited to the migrants to California during that period, but some of it was undoubtedly due to the preponderance of newcomers from states which were in the traditionally Democratic South.

In the period from 1920 to 1930 the increase in registrations to vote in California was in almost exactly the same proportions as the increase in population. That is, slightly more than 60 per cent increase in each. From 1930 to 1940, the increase in voting registrations was somewhat spectacular. While the population increased only slightly more than 20 per cent, voting registrations increased by 80 per cent.[48] But even more spectacular was the increase in Democratic party registration by 431 per cent in that same period. Perhaps part of the increase in registrations to vote was due to the frequent use of registration certificates as a means of proving residence for the purpose of securing relief or for civil service jobs requiring proof of residence.[49]

Reference to the Statement of the Vote of California, which is issued following each election by the California Secretary of State, shows the Republican party candidates usually received a majority of the votes cast until the advent of the Progressive Republican group in 1912, when that party became the leading party in the state. After the reunion of the Republican branches, that party again came to the front. In the Presidential Election of 1932, the Democratic electors received a large majority vote, as did the Democratic candidate for Senator from California. The trend, however, was almost reversed in the General Election of 1934 in the vote for Governor and Lieutenant-Governor; and Hiram W. Johnson-- long-time Republican and Progressive party man was returned to the United States Senate by a combination of various parties.

Culbert L. Olson was elected Governor on the Democratic ticket in 1938, showing the new Democratic party strength. Actual votes cast, however, did not give the Democrats a majority comparable to that shown by party registrations.[50]

Although Democratic Presidential Electors were chosen in 1940, Hiram W. Hohnson again showed his personal popularity when he won re-nomination to the Senate on Republican, Democratic and Progressive party tickets and was elected without serious opposition in the General Election.[51]

Voters' registrations may indicate the potential strength of a political party. Beginning in 1922, the Secretary of State included in his Statement of the Vote the number of voters registered in each county by political party affiliation. In 1922 there were more than three Republican registrations to one Democratic registration among the qualifying voters of California. This proportion was maintained until 1932, when the Democratic party more than doubled in registrations within a two-year period. The Republican party showed a slight loss at that time, although they still led by 400,000 registrations.[52]

The Democrats continued to gain materially in number of registered voters for each election on through the decade. The Democratic vote, however, did not keep pace with the registrations. In the election of 1938, there were 2,144,360 registered Democrats, but the Democratic candidates for Governor and United States Senator polled respectively 1,391,734 and 1,372,314 votes. Compared with that were only 1,293,929 registered Republicans, while the Republican candidate for Governor received 1,171,019 votes and the Republican candidate for United States Senator netted 1,126,240 votes in the General Election.[53]

Considering the number of migrants to California from traditionally Democratic states, and comparing the Democratic and Republican votes in the election of 1938, it appeared that these newcomers may have polled the deciding votes in that election.

CONCLUSION

The migration to California from 1930 to 1940, while not precedent-breaking in either numbers or per cent of increase, was of great importance, both to California and to the nation.

Rural "slum-housing" conditions brought increased health problems. Unpredictable school enrollments, unduly large relief rolls, and unprecedented demands on the public health facilities increased the burden of the taxpayer. Segregation of large groups of low-income groups made for poor social adjustment within the various communities.

Assistance from the federal government was necessary, both in terms of money and in planning on a nation-wide scale to prevent an increase in the problem.

Finally, the migration of a large group from the "Solid South" was an influence in the changing political picture in California.

While none of the above conditions can be traced wholly to the migration, it did play a part in all of them.

Footnotes--Chapter VI

[1] Carey McWilliams, _Factories in the Field_.

[2] U.S., 75th Congress, 3d Session, Senate Special Committee to Investigate Unemployment and Relief, "Extract from Hearings," 1159.

[3] Harrison S. Robinson, California State Chamber of Commerce, "California Faces the Migrant Problem", Address.

[4] Calif., State Emergency Relief Admin., "Survey of Agricultural Labor Requirements in California, 1935," 8.

[5] Rowell, "Drought Refugee," op. cit., 1361.

[6] Tolan Committee, VI, 2753.

[7] Ibid., 2840.

[8] U.S. 75th Congress, 3d Session, Senate, op. cit., 1159.

[9] "Government Camps for Agricultural Workers," U.S. Department of Labor, _Monthly Labor Review_, L (March, 1940), 625.

[10] Laurence I. Hewes, Jr., "Report before the Subcommittee of the Committee on Education and Labor."
The relief agencies defined a "resident" as a person who had established residence in the state and county of application and met all legal residence requirements for receiving assistance from any of the regularly established agencies. A "transient" was defined as a person having legal residence in some other county or state. A "homeless" person was one who had no legal residence. If he had resided in the state for a year, and had resided in more than one county, he was classed "state homeless," or if he had residence in no other state he was identified as a "federal homeless."

[11]The "private" agencies consisted of the social work agencies maintained by the Protestant, Catholic, and Jewish organizations, the Red Cross, Travelers' Aid, and similar groups. There was a six-page directory of such agencies in Los Angeles, and similar directories in other cities.

[12]H. Dewey Anderson, State Relief Administration, "Who Are on Relief in California?"

[13]Ante, 22.

[14]"Grapes of Joy--'Okies' Forge Ahead," Current History, LI (March, 1940), 48-49.

[15]"Private Homesteads for the Okies," Business Week, March 9, 1940, 24-26.

[16]"Okies Interest Banks," Business Week, April 6, 1940, 24-26.

[17]Hazel Hendricks, "Farmers Without Farms," The Atlantic Monthly, CLXVI (October, 1940), 461.

[18]Tolan Committee, Interstate Migration, V, 2122.

[19]Frank J. Taylor, "California's 'Grapes of Wrath,'" Forum, CII (November, 1939), 232-238; Carey McWilliams, "California's Migrants," Ibid., CIII (December, 1939), 7. A reply to Taylor.

[20]"Wrath on Both Sides," Forum, CIII (January, 1940), 24-25.

[21]Carleton Beals, "Migs--American Shantytown on Wheels," The Forum and Century, XCIX (January, 1938), 10.

[22]National Resources Committee, "Farm Tenancy," Report of the President's Committee. Picture supplement.

[23]Calif., Division of Immigration and Housing, "Memorandum on Housing ... in California."

[24]Carleton Beals, "Migs--American Shantytown on Wheels," The Forum and Century, XCIC (January, 1938), 10.

[25]Fresno, Bee, February 26, 1941.

[26]"I Wonder Where We Can Go Now," Fortune, XIX (April, 1939), 91.

[27]"The Farm Transient," Newsweek, March 6, 1939.

[28]Laurence I. Newes, Jr., "Report before the Subcommittee of the Committee on Education and Labor."

[29] Ibid.

[30] U.S. Dept. of Agriculture, Farm Security Admin., "Migrant Farm Labor," 8.

[31] Ibid., 9.

[32] Hewes, Jr. op. cit.

[33] "I Wonder Where We Can Go Now," op. cit., 119.

[34] Tolan Com., VIII, op. cit., 3292.

[35] U.S. Dept. of Agric., FSA, op. cit., 13.

[36] "I Wonder Where ...," op. cit.; "No Jobs in Calif., op. cit., CCXI, 28.

[37] U.S. Dept. of Agric., op. cit., 13.

[38] Hewes, op. cit.

[39] Esther A. Canter, "California 'Renovates' the Dust-Bowler," Hygeia, XVIII (May, 1940), 420-423.

[40] Tolan Com., Interstate op. cit., VI, 2512.

[41] Hewes, op. cit.

[42] Tolan Com., op. cit., 2433.

[43] Ibid., 2434.

[44] Ibid., 2436.

[45] Ibid., 2435.

[46] Ibid., 2436.

[47] Ibid., 2438

[48] Calif. Secretary of State, Statement of the Vote, General Elections, 1910-1940.

[49] It is known that in some cases persons registered as voters upon arrival in California and combined this with forged documents to prove they were state residents and entitled to relief, or eligible for civil service examinations requiring local residence. General dissatisfaction with the federal government, because of the depression which was being attributed to President Hoover, caused many voters to change their registration. Even greater changes in party registration occurred,

however, after 1933 when federal relief agencies were created. Voter's registration certificates were produced by some of the jobless to show that they were "properly" registered, as it was commonly believed that political affiliation influenced assignment to the work-relief program, or even the securing of general relief. This may explain part of the great increase in Democratic registrations and the comparatively small vote for Democratic candidates in the elections.

[50] Calif., Secy. of State, Statement of the Vote, op. cit., 1938.

[51] Ibid., 1940.

[52] Ibid., 1922-1932.

[53] Ibid., 1938.

BIBLIOGRAPHY

"Agricultural Labor Contractor System in California," U.S. Department of Labor, Monthly Labor Review, LII (February, 1941), 345-348.

Anderson, H. Dewey, State Relief Administration. "Who Are on Relief in California?" San Francisco, 1939.
    A mimeographed report by the Administrator of the California State Relief Administration to the staff.

Bancroft, Hubert Howe. History of California, VII, 1860-1890. San Francisco, 1890.

Beals, Carleton. "Migs: America's Shantytown on Wheels," The Forum and Century, XCIX (January, 1938), 10-15.

Beard, Charles A. and Mary R. Beard, A Basic History of the United States. New York, 1944.

California, Board of Control. California and the Oriental. Sacramento, 1921.
    A report to Governor Stephens on June 19, 1920.

_____, Division of Immigration and Housing. Memorandum on Housing Conditions Among Migratory Workers in California. Los Angeles, 1939.

_____, Governor C. C. Young's Fact Finding Committee. Mexicans in California. San Francisco, 1930.

_____, Secretary of State. Statement of the Vote. Sacramento, 1910-1940.
    These reports are published following each election. The reports for each General (November) Election between the dates noted were used.

_____, State Emergency Relief Administration. "Survey of Agricultural Labor Requirements in California, 1935." N.P., 1936.

_____, State Emergency Relief Administration. Transients in California, 1936. n.p., 1936.

_____, State Relief Administration, Migratory Labor in California. n.p., 1936.

_____, State Relief Administration. Review of Activities of the State Relief Administration of California, 1933-35. Sacramento, 1936.

"California: No Hobo Utopia," Literary Digest, CXXI (February 15, 1936), 9.

Canter, Esther A., "California 'Renovates' the Dust-Bowler," Hygeia, XVIII (May, 1940), 420-423.

Cross, William T. "The Poor Migrant in California," Social Forces, XV (March, 1937), 423-427.

_____ and Dorothy E. Cross. Newcomers and Nomads in California. Stanford University, 1937.

"Flee Dustbowl for California," Business Week, IX (July 3, 1937), 36-37.

"Government Camps for Agricultural Workers," U.S. Department of Labor, Monthly Labor Review, L (March, 1940), 625-627.

"Grapes of Joy, Okies Forge Ahead," Current History, LI (March, 1940), 48-49
        Condensed from a dispatch from Salinas, California to the Christian Science Monitor.

Henderson, Carolina A. "Letters from the Dust Bowl." The Atlantic Monthly, XLVII (May, 1936), 540-551.
        For twenty-eight years Mrs. Henderson and her husband had been farming in Oklahoma. For the five years ending 1936, their household was one of those that fought the drought and dust storms. These letters were written to a friend in Maryland between June, 1935 and March, 1936.

Hendricks, Hazel. "Farmers Without Farms." The Atlantic Monthly, CLXVI (October, 1940), 461-468.
        Miss Hendricks was Field Consultant to the United States Children's Bureau.

Hewes, Laurence I., Jr. "Report Before the Sub-Committee of the Committee on Education and Labor." San Francisco, 1940.
        Mr. Hewes was the Director of the Farm Security Administration, Region IX, at San Francisco. This was a mimeographed copy of a report made by him.

"I Wonder Where We Can Go Now," Fortune, XIX (April, 1939), 91-120

Lange, Dorothea, and Paul S. Taylor. An American Exodus: A Record of Human Erosion. New York, 1939.
        Excellent photographs and text. Mr. Taylor is Professor Economics at the University of California. Miss Lange took the pictures which tell their own unforgettable story of the migrants.

Los Angeles, Herald-Express. May 17, 21; August 24; and December 11, 1935; February 4-5, 1936.

_____, Police Department. Transiency in Southern California. Los Angeles, 1937.

Mears, Eliot Grinnell, <u>Resident Orientals on the American Pacific Coast</u>. New York, 1927.

McWilliams, Carey. "California's Migrants," Forum, CII (December, 1939), 7.
         A reply to Frank J. Taylor's "California's 'Grapes of Wrath'" in the November, 1939, <u>Forum</u>.

McWilliams, Carey. <u>Factories in the Field</u>. Boston, 1939.

Niklason, C.R. <u>Commercial Survey of the Pacific Southwest</u>. Washington, 1930.

"No Jobs in California." <u>Saturday Evening Post</u>, CCII (November 12, 1938), 18-40.

"Okies Interest Banks." <u>Business Week</u>, April 6, 1940, 24-26.

"Private Homesteads for the Okies." <u>Business Week</u>, March 9, 1940, 24-26.

Robinson, Harrison S. "California Faces the Migrant Problem." San Francisco, 1939.
         An address given at San Francisco on November 30, 1939, by Mr. Robinson, Director and Chairman of the Special Committee on the Migrant Problem of the California State Chamber of Commerce.

Rowell, Edward J. "Drought Refugee and Labor Migration to California in 1936." U.S. Department of Labor, <u>Monthly Labor Review</u>, XLIII (December, 1936), 1355-1363.

Smith, Wallace. <u>Garden of the Sun: A History of San Joaquin Valley from 1772 to 1939</u>. Los Angeles, 1939.

Spry, William. "Homestead and Exemption Laws." <u>Encyclopedia Brittannica</u>, 14th edition, XI, 704-705. New York, 1937.

Steinbeck, John. <u>The Grapes of Wrath</u>. New York, 1939.
         Pulitzer Prize winning, and best-selling novel about the migrants in California.

Taylor, Frank J. "California's 'Grapes of Wrath,'" Forum, CII (November, 1939), 232-238.

Taylor, Paul S. <u>Mexican Labor in the United States</u>. Berkeley, 1936.

Taylor, Paul S., and Edward J. Rowell. "Refugee Labor Migration to California, 1937," U.S. Department of Labor, <u>Monthly Labor Review</u>, XLVII (August, 1938), 240-250.

Taylor, Paul S., and Tom Vasey. "Drought Refugee and Labor Migration to California, June-December, 1935," U.S. Department of Labor, <u>Monthly Labor Review</u>, XLII (February, 1936), 312-318.

"The Farm Transient," Newsweek, March 6, 1937.

"The Grasslands," Fortune, XII (November, 1935), 59-67, 185-190, 198, 200, 203.

"The Okies--A National Problem," Business Week, February 10, 1940, 17.

"These Pictures Prove Facts in Grapes of Wrath," Life, February 19, 1940.

Tolan Committee, Interstate Migration. Washington, 1941.
     See U.S., 76th Congress, 3d Session, House Select Committee.

U.S. Bureau of the Census, Ninth Census: 1870, I, III, Washington, 1872.

_____, Eleventh Census: 1890. Washington, 1893.

_____, Twelfth Census: 1900, I. Washington, 1901.

_____, Fourteenth Census: 1920, I, II, III, V. Washington, 1922.

_____, Fifteenth Census: 1930, I, III. Washington, 1931-32.

_____, Sixteenth Census: 1940. Reports on Population, I, II; Reports on Agri-
culture, Irrigation and Drainage, I. Washington, 1943.

U.S., Department of Agriculture, Farm Security Administration. "A Chart showing
individuals entering California in automobiles' in search of manual employment' 1935-1941." San Francisco, n.d.
     A one-page mimeographed compilation of figures from the border check
stations.

_____, A Study of 6655 Migrant Households Receiving Emergency Grants, Farm
Security Administration, California, 1938. San Francisco, 1939.

_____, "Health for Western Farm Workers." San Francisco, 1941.
     A mimeographed report on health services.

_____, "Migrant Farm Labor--The Problem and Some Efforts to Meet It." Wash-
ington, 1940.

_____, "Mobile Camps for Migrant Farm Families." n.p., 1940.

U.S., Department of Labor, Bureau of Immigration. Annual Report of the Commissioner-General of Immigration to the Secretary of Labor. Washington,
1903-1931.
     Fiscal years 1902-1903 to 1930-1931. Printed reports issued each year,
giving full statistics on immigration and emigration.

U.S., National Resources Committee. <u>Farm Tenancy</u>. Washington, 1937.
        A report of the President's Committee. Contains an excellent picture
supplement.

U.S., 61st Congress, 3d Session, Senate. <u>Report of the Immigration Commission</u>,
    I. Washington, 1911.

_____, 75th Congress, 3d Session, Senate. "Extract from Hearings Before a
Special Committee to Investigate Unemployment and Relief." Washington,
1938.

_____, 76th Congress, 3d Session, House Select Committee to Investigate the
Interstate Migration of Destitute Citizens, <u>Interstate Migration</u>. Washington,
1941.
        Representative John. H. Tolan of California was Chairman of the com-
mittee, which was commonly referred to as the "Tolan Committee". Hearings were held at New York City; Montgomery, Alabama; Chicago, Illinois;
Lincoln, Nebraska; Oklahoma City, Oklahoma; San Francisco and Los
Angeles, California; and Washington, D.C., in the years 1940 and 1941.
Many migrants and other citizens from the various states as well as officials
of local, state and federal governments testified before this committee. It
is the greatest single compilation of materials on the migrant problem for
the period.

"Wrath on Both Sides," <u>Forum</u>, CIII (January, 1940), 24-25.
        Letters from readers, commenting on articles by Frank J. Taylor and
Carey McWilliams.